LET'S INVESTIGATE SCIENCE
SCIENCE
The Night Sky

LET'S INVESTIGATE SCIENCE
The Night Sky

Robin Kerrod

Illustrated by Terry Hadler

BENCHMARK BOOKS

MARSHALL CAVENDISH
NEW YORK

Library Edition Published 1996

Benchmark Books
Marshall Cavendish Corporation
99 White Plains Road
Tarrytown, New York 10591

© Marshall Cavendish Corporation 1996

Series created by Graham Beehag Books

Library of Congress Cataloging-in-Publication Data
Kerrod, Robin.
    The night sky / Robin Kerrod : illustrated by Terry Hadler
     p. cm. – (Lets investigate science)
    Includes bibliographical references and index.
    Summary: Describes what stars and constellations can be seen in
    the night sky and provides instructions for finding them.
    ISBN 0-7614-0029-X (lib. bdg.)
    1. Astronomy – Juvenile literature. 2. Astronomy – Observers' manuals –
    Juvenile literature. [1. Astronomy – Observers' manuals.]
    I. Hadler, Terry. II. Title. III. Series: Kerrod, Robin.
    Let's investigate science.
    QB46,K425 1996
    520–dc20   95-16534
                                         CIP
                                         AC

MCC Editorial Consultant: Marvin Tolman, Ed.D.
                    Brigham Young University

Printed in Hong Kong

Contents

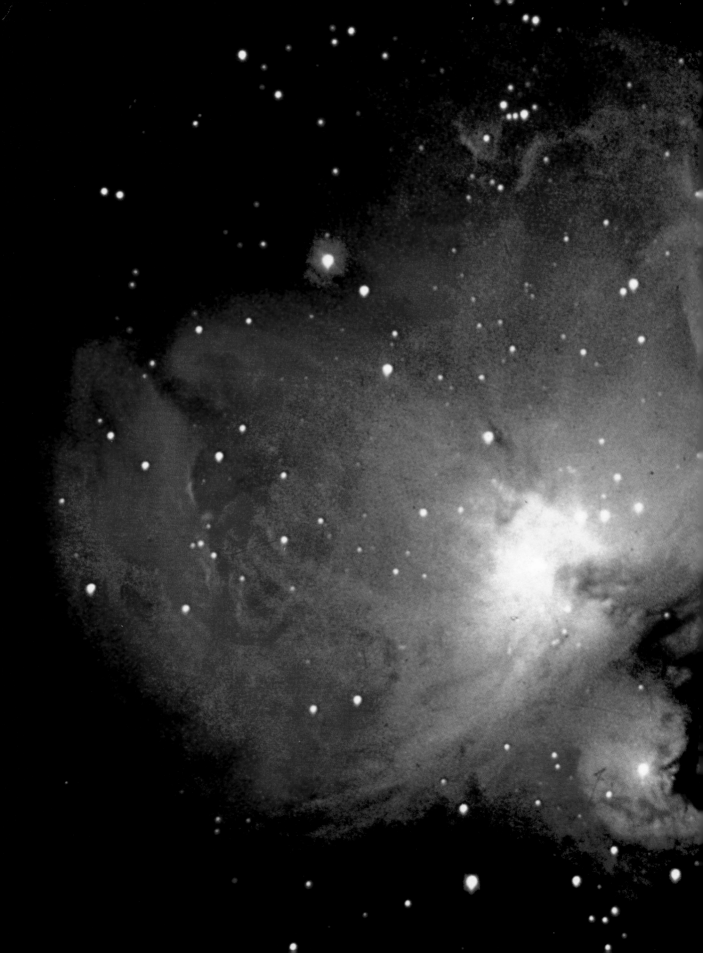

Introduction

Out in the country, away from city lights, you can see a magnificent spectacle almost every night. It is the spectacle of the starry heavens. Thousands upon thousands of stars shine down on the darkened Earth. They twinkle and sparkle like jewels nestling in black velvet.

Humans have been fascinated by the heavens from earliest times. They watched and wondered and tried to explain what they saw. They came to believe that the heavens in some way affected people's lives here on Earth. This belief is known as astrology.

The ancient astrologers observed the skies carefully, looking for signs that might tell them what the future held for people on Earth. Their observations paved the way for the true scientific study of the heavens, which we call astronomy.

Astronomers study all the bodies that appear in the skies – stars, planets, moons, meteors, and comets. In this book we investigate stellar astronomy, the astronomy of the stars. We look at the patterns they make in the night sky. We examine what stars are like. We see how they gather into great star islands traveling through space, and how multitudes of these star islands make up a vast Universe.

> You can check your answers to the questions, investigations, and workouts featured throughout this book on pages 60-62.

◀ Some night-sky features, such as the distinctively red Great Nebula in Orion, can be found by using a telescope or binoculars.

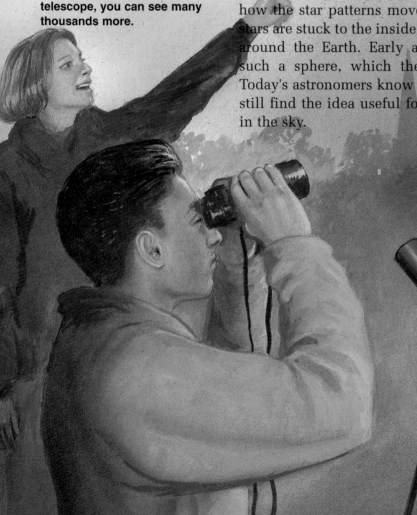

1 The Starry Heavens

◀ This picture was taken with a camera that turns at the same slow speed as the stars appear to move in the night sky. An artificial satellite appears as a long, curving trail against the stars and clusters of the Milky Way.

▼ When you look up at the sky on a dark night, you can see thousands upon thousands of stars. If you look at the sky through binoculars or a telescope, you can see many thousands more.

At first sight, the night sky looks much the same in all directions, just a confusing mass of stars, some bright, some dim. But if you keep stargazing for a while, you will notice that each part of the sky looks different from every other part. The bright stars in each part form different patterns, which we call constellations. We use these star patterns to find our way around the sky.

If you keep stargazing for a long time, you will notice how the star patterns move overhead. It appears as if the stars are stuck to the inside of a great sphere that is rotating around the Earth. Early astronomers thought there was such a sphere, which they called the celestial sphere. Today's astronomers know there is no such thing, but they still find the idea useful for locating the positions of stars in the sky.

10

The Big Dipper

Patterns in the sky

On a dark night if you look toward the north, you will see quite a few bright stars in the sky. If you look in the same direction at about the same time the following night, you will see that the bright stars are in roughly the same positions. After a few nights' stargazing, you will learn to recognize the patterns these bright stars make – the constellations.

In the summer, looking toward the northwest at about 11 p.m., you can see the pattern of bright stars shown above. If you join up the stars, you get a shape like a cup with a long handle. Years ago people used cups like this to dip into water and milk and called them dippers. For this reason, the star pattern came to be called the Big Dipper.

▼ When a few extra lines are added to join the stars, the shape of a dipper becomes apparent.

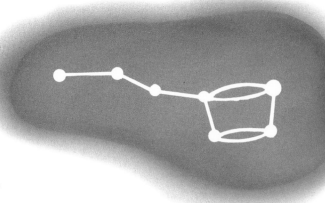

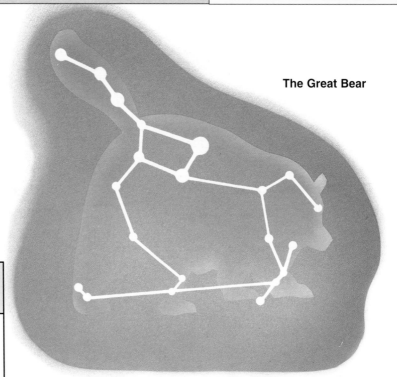

The Great Bear

INVESTIGATE

Join the Dots

There are two other patterns of stars illustrated below that you can see in the night sky at different times of the year. Trace diagrams 1. and 2. and then connect the stars in any way you want, and see if you can make them into the shapes of animals. Use plenty of imagination! Then look at the Answers on page 60 to see how ancient astronomers pictured these star patterns.

Another name for this star pattern is the Plow, because it looks like the handle and blade of an early horse-drawn plow. Astronomers find it useful to identify the constellations by names that are suggested by the arrangement of their bright stars, although the shapes of these descriptive names are not always obvious.

Ancient astronomers saw the stars in the Big Dipper as part of a much larger star pattern, or constellation. They thought this larger pattern looked like a large bear, so they called it the Great Bear.

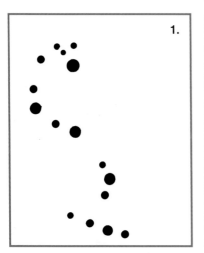

1.

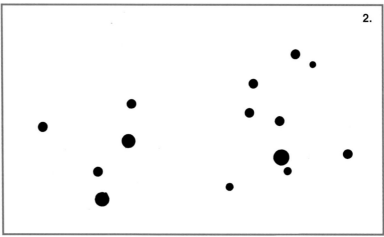

2.

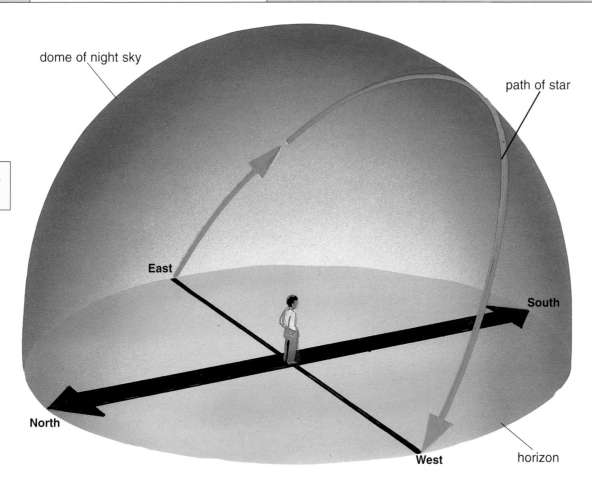

dome of night sky

path of star

East

South

North

West

horizon

The dome of the heavens

With a little imagination, we can picture the heavens as a huge, dark dome above our heads. The stars seem to be attached to the inside of this dome.

But the dome itself isn't fixed. If you keep stargazing for a while, you notice that the patterns of stars slowly change their position. The whole dome of the sky seems to be moving. It seems to be moving from east to west.

If you look toward the east, you can see the stars rising (appearing) there. Then they slowly climb through the sky, moving toward the west. They reach their highest point in the sky in the south. Afterward, they slowly descend and eventually set (disappear) below the horizon in the west.

If you look toward the east on two consecutive nights at about the same time, you will see that the same stars are rising. In other words, the dome of the heavens spins around once a day.

▲The dome of the night sky whirls overhead every night. The stars appear to rise above the eastern horizon and set below the western horizon.

INVESTIGATE

Watching the stars whirl

You can see how the stars appear to move through the sky by taking photographs. You need only simple photographic equipment: a camera with a setting for time exposures, a tripod, and a cable release to work the camera shutter.

Set up the camera on the tripod and point it to any part of the sky, tilting it upward at an angle of about 45 degrees. Make sure there are no house lights or street lights nearby.

Set the camera for time exposure, and open the shutter using the cable release. This keeps you from shaking the camera when you open the shutter. Keep the shutter open for about half an hour. Then close the shutter using the cable release again.

Point the camera at another part of the sky and repeat the procedure. Using a compass, position the camera so it is facing north. Then repeat the procedure again.

When you get your photographs developed, you will see that the stars have made trails. This shows that they are moving in relation to the Earth.

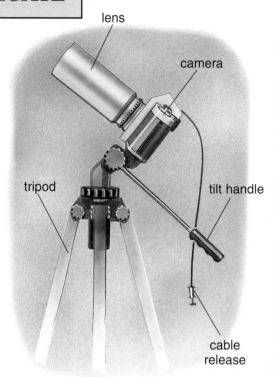

lens

camera

tripod

tilt handle

cable release

The celestial sphere

There is a dome of the heavens above our heads wherever we live on Earth. In other words, the Earth seems to be at the center of a great dark sphere. We call it the celestial (heavenly) sphere. The stars seem to be stuck on the inside of this sphere. As we have seen, the sphere spins around from east to west once a day. We can picture the celestial sphere like this:

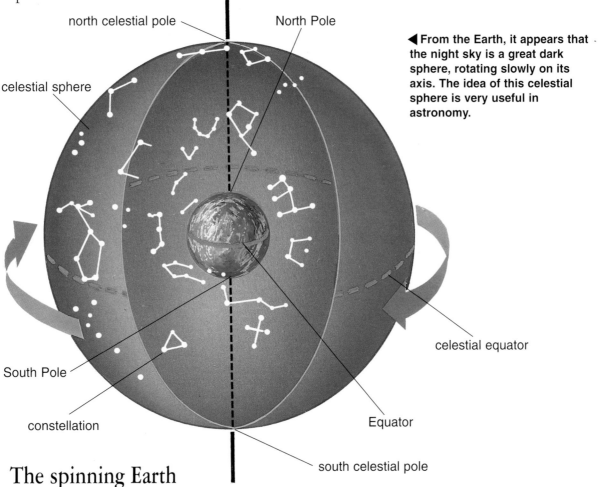

north celestial pole

North Pole

celestial sphere

◀ From the Earth, it appears that the night sky is a great dark sphere, rotating slowly on its axis. The idea of this celestial sphere is very useful in astronomy.

celestial equator

South Pole

constellation

Equator

south celestial pole

The spinning Earth

In fact there is no such thing as a celestial sphere spinning around the Earth. The apparent spinning of the heavens from east to west is caused by the Earth spinning around on its own axis in the opposite direction. The Earth's axis is an imaginary line going through the Earth from the North Pole to the South Pole.

Q What is the most noticeable effect of the Earth spinning on its axis?

At the Poles

The celestial sphere appears to spin around on an axis that goes through the north and south celestial poles. These poles are located directly above the Earth's North and South Poles.

   If you stood at the North Pole and looked straight up, the stars would appear to travel in circles around the north celestial pole. If you stood at the South Pole, the stars would appear to circle around the south celestial pole. The stars circling the north celestial pole appear to travel in the opposite direction from the stars circling the south celestial pole.

Q **1.** The diagrams on the right show the path of the stars around the north celestial pole and the south celestial pole. which diagram is which?

Q **2.** If you stood at the North Pole and looked east, in which direction would the stars be moving? Draw a sketch to illustrate your answer.

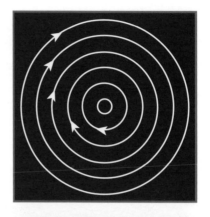

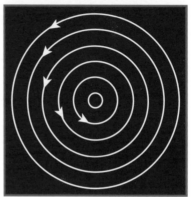

15

At the Equator

If you stood on the Equator and looked at the sky, you would see the stars moving in a different way. The celestial poles now lie on the horizon (see diagram).

Q **3.** In which direction would the stars move if you looked toward (**1**) the east, (**2**) the west? Draw sketches to illustrate your answer.

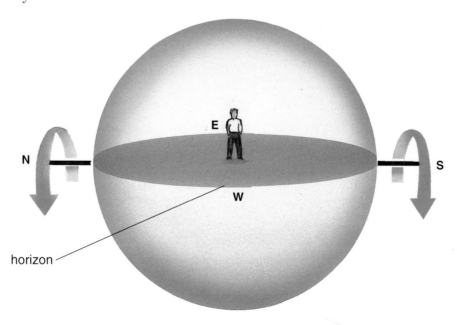

horizon

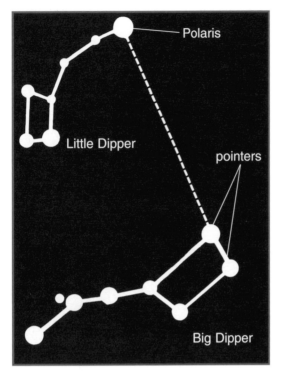

Pole star

If you look at the picture on the left again, you will notice that there is a bright star in the center. It has hardly moved at all. This is because it is located almost exactly in the same position as the north celestial pole. We often call this star the North Star or the Pole Star. Astronomers call it Polaris.

Polaris is a useful aid for finding your way at night because it always stays in the same position in the northern sky.

Polaris is part of a constellation known as the Little Bear. The main stars in this constellation form a shape much like the Big Dipper, and it is called the Little Dipper.

Like the other stars in the Little Dipper, Polaris is fainter than the stars in the Big Dipper. We can find it easily because two stars in the Big Dipper point toward it. We call these stars the Pointers.

OBSERVATION

In this observation exercise, you must look at the Big Dipper in the northern sky at different times of the year, in mid-March (spring), mid-June (summer), mid-September (fall), and mid-December (winter). Make your observations on the same day of the month, say the 15th, and at the same time, say 11 p.m. Sketch which way up the Big Dipper appears in the heavens.

The diagram shows the positions of the Big Dipper in the night sky at about 11 p.m. on the 15th of March, June, September, and December. From your sketches, which positions in the diagram relate to which times of the year?

Star trails

When you take a photograph of the night sky, looking north and centering the North Star, you get a picture like the one above. The stars make circular trails because of the spinning of the celestial sphere (or, the Earth).

If you could photograph the heavens for 24 hours, you would find that the trail made by each star would be a complete circle. The center of each circle marks the position of the celestial north pole.

Q Why can't you photograph the starry skies for 24 hours at a time?

▲ This is a long-exposure photograph of the night sky taken with a fixed camera. The camera was pointing toward the North Star. The stars show up as curved streaks of light because the heavens seem to be moving in relation to the Earth.

Celestial signposts

We saw on the last page that a pair of stars in the Big Dipper point toward Polaris, the Pole Star. We are in effect using the Big Dipper as a celestial signpost, to help find our way around the heavens.

Other stars in the Big Dipper help us find stars in other constellations, too. For example, if you follow the curve of the handle away from the cup, the first bright star you come to is Arcturus, in the constellation Boötes.

Signpost Orion

One of the best signposts in the heavens is the constellation Orion. It has a distinctive shape marked by bright stars, so it is easy to spot. The diagram below shows how useful it is in identifying other bright stars.

Q Which of the stars in the diagram below is best known? Why?

▼ The constellation Orion helps you identify many other stars and constellations. They include Capella, in the constellation Auriga, the Pleiades cluster and Aldebaran in Taurus, Sirius in Canis Major, Procyon in Canis Minor, and Castor and Pollux in Gemini. Orion is especially useful as a signpost because it can be seen from both northern and southern hemispheres some time during the year.

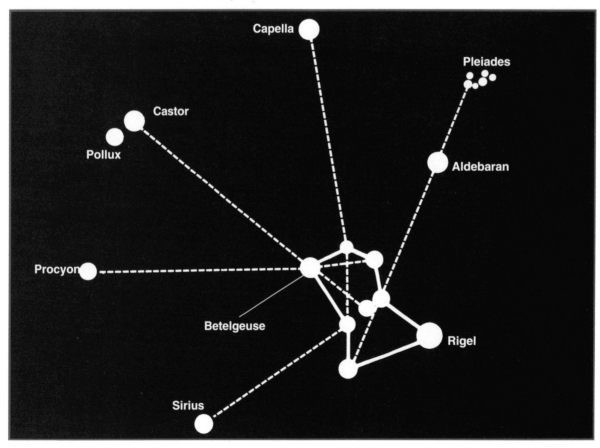

The celestial hemispheres

We saw earlier how we can imagine the heavens as a huge celestial sphere surrounding the Earth. We can split it into two celestial hemispheres at the celestial equator. The celestial equator is an imaginary line in the heavens directly above the Earth's Equator.

On the next two pages, we identify the constellations that appear in the northern and the southern celestial hemispheres.

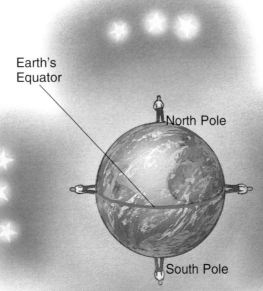

Earth's Equator
North Pole
South Pole

orthern constellations
nothern celestial hemisphere
arth's quator
southern constellations
southern celestial hemisphere

Different points of view

Because the Earth is round, observers in different parts of the world see different parts of the celestial sphere. Observers near the North Pole, for example, will be able to see the stars of the northern hemisphere, but they won't be able to see the stars of the southern hemisphere, and vice versa.

Observers in other locations will be able to see some of the stars of both hemispheres. Observers in Florida, for example, will during the year be able to see all the stars of the northern hemisphere and many of the stars of the southern hemisphere.

Q Fill in the missing words in this statement. If I lived at the Equator, I would during the year see ..... of the constellations of the northern hemisphere and ..... of the constellations of the southern hemisphere.

Naming the constellations

The Big Dipper forms part of the constellation of the Great Bear. "Great Bear" is the common name for the constellation. Astronomers call it Ursa Major, the Latin for Great Bear. In fact, they call all the constellations by their Latin names. The constellations we commonly call the Lion and the Bull, for example, are Leo and Taurus, respectively, in Latin.

The ancient Greeks named most of the constellations more than 2,000 years ago. They named them after figures – animals, gods, heroes, kings, and queens – that appeared in their mythology. They made up stories about how these figures came to appear in the heavens.

20

KEY

1 Andromeda	**31 Cygnus**, Swan	**61 Pavo**, Peacock
2 Antlia, Air Pump	**32 Delphinus**, Dolphin	**62 Pegasus**, Flying Horse
3 Apus, Bird of Paradise	**33 Dorado**, Swordfish	**63 Perseus**
4 Aquarius, Water-Bearer	**34 Draco**, Dragon	**64 Phoenix**
5 Aquila, Eagle	**35 Equuleus**, Foal	**65 Pictor**, Painter
6 Ara, Altar	**36 Eridanus**	**66 Pisces**, Fishes
7 Aries, Ram	**37 Fornax**, Furnace	**67 Piscis Austrinus**, Southern Fish
8 Auriga, Charioteer	**38 Gemini**, Twins	**68 Puppis**, Poop
9 Boötes, Herdsman	**39 Grus**, Crane	**69 Pyxis**, Compass
10 Caelum, Chisel	**40 Hercules**	**70 Reticulum**, Net
11 Camelopardalis, Giraffe	**41 Horologium**, Clock	**71 Sagitta**, Arrow
12 Cancer, Crab	**42 Hydra**, Water Snake	**72 Sagittarius**, Archer
13 Canes Venatici, Hunting Dogs	**43 Hydrus**, Little Snake	**73 Scorpius**, Scorpion
14 Canis Major, Great Dog	**44 Indus**, Indian	**74 Sculptor**
15 Canis Minor, Little Dog	**45 Lacerta**, Lizard	**75 Scutum**, Shield
16 Capricornus, Sea Goat	**46 Leo**, Lion	**76 Serpens**, Serpent
17 Carina, Keel	**47 Leo Minor**, Little Lion	**77 Sextans**, Sextant
18 Cassiopeia	**48 Lepus**, Hare	**78 Taurus**, Bull
19 Centaurus, Centaur	**49 Libra**, Scales	**79 Telescopium**, Telescope
20 Cepheus	**50 Lupus**, Wolf	**80 Triangulum**, Triangle
21 Cetus, Whale	**51 Lynx**	**81 Triangulum Australe**, Southern Triangle
22 Chamaeleon, Chameleon	**52 Lyra**, Lyre	**82 Tucana**, Toucan
23 Circinus, Compasses	**53 Mensa**, Table	**83 Ursa Major**, Great Bear
24 Columba, Dove	**54 Microscopium**, Microscope	**84 Ursa Minor**, Little Bear
25 Coma Berenices, Berenice's Hair	**55 Monoceros**, Unicorn	**85 Vela**, Sails
26 Corona Australis, Southern Crown	**56 Musca**, Fly	**86 Virgo**, Virgin
27 Corona Borealis, Northern Crown	**57 Norma**, Rule	**87 Volans**, Flying Fish
28 Corvus, Crow	**58 Octans**, Octant	**88 Vulpecula**, Fox
29 Crater, Cup	**59 Ophiuchus**, Serpent-Bearer	
30 Crux, Southern Cross	**60 Orion**	

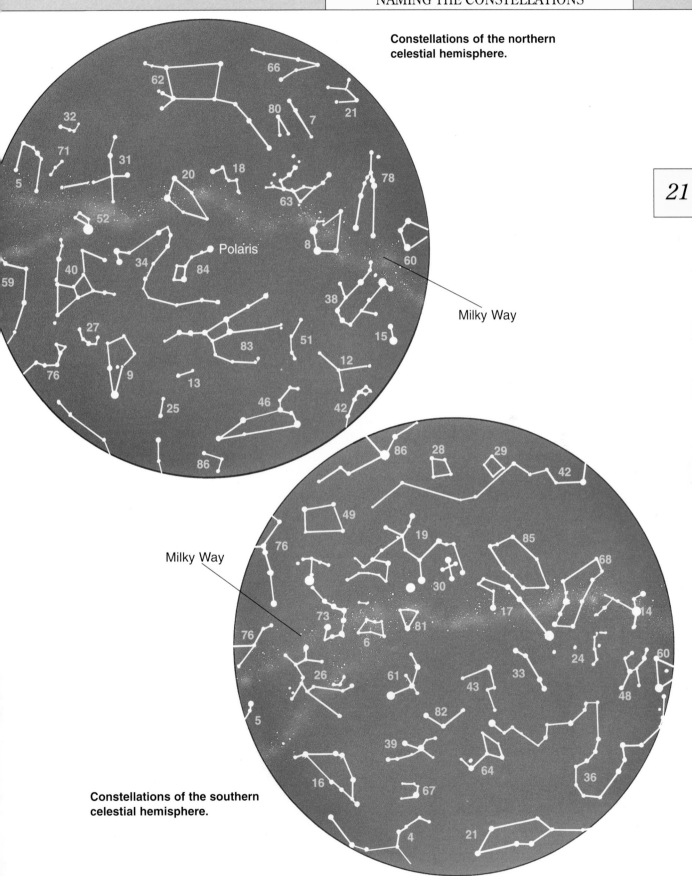

Constellations of the northern celestial hemisphere.

Polaris

Milky Way

Milky Way

Constellations of the southern celestial hemisphere.

The changing heavens

The Earth moves in orbit around the Sun, taking a year to complete a full circle, but viewed from the Earth, it is the Sun that seems to be moving. It seems to be moving through the heavens against the background of stars.

Q How long does it take the Sun to make a full circle of the heavens?

Disappearing constellations

At any time, you can't see the stars in the part of the heavens the Sun is passing through because the Sun's light is too bright. In other words, you can't see certain constellations at certain times of the year.

Or, put another way, different constellations appear in the heavens at different times of the year. On pages 24 through 27, we look at the difference in the appearance of the heavens between winter and summer.

Ecliptic and zodiac

The path the Sun follows around the celestial sphere each year is called the ecliptic. It passes through 12 constellations. They are called the constellations of the zodiac. The planets also travel through these constellations. That is because they travel around the Sun in much the same plane (flat surface) as the Earth does.

▼ **The twelve constellations of the zodiac, or "star signs". The positions of the planets in these constellations are considered important in astrology. They are believed to affect people's lives.**

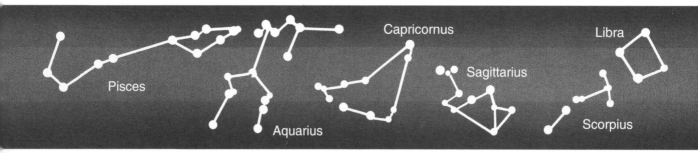

Pisces

Aquarius

Capricornus

Sagittarius

Scorpius

Libra

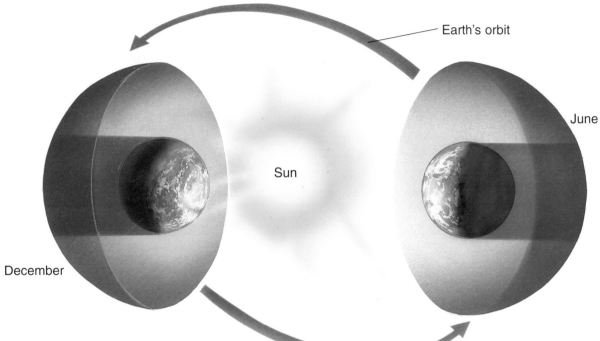

Earth's orbit

June

Sun

December

▲ The light from the Sun blots out certain constellations as it appears to travel around the celestial sphere. At the end of June, for example, you won't be able to see Gemini because the Sun is passing through this constellation at the time. And in early December, you won't be able to see Scorpius on the opposite side of the celestial sphere because by then the Sun will be passing through that constellation.

▶ The ideas of astrology entered other fields of knowledge, including medicine. The signs of the zodiac were thought to affect different organs of the body.

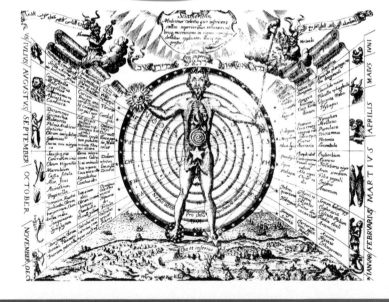

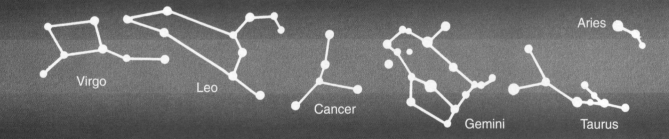

Virgo

Leo

Cancer

Gemini

Aries

Taurus

Winter stars

Looking north

The Big Dipper lies toward the east, with the handle almost vertical. Its two pointer stars point toward Polaris and beyond to the unmistakable W-shape of Cassiopeia. If the skies are really dark, you can see that Cassiopeia lies in a faintly glowing band: this is the Milky Way.

Low in the west is a square pattern of stars. This is the Square of Pegasus. Roughly midway between the Square and Cassiopeia, in the constellation Andromeda, is a fuzzy patch of light. It is a nearby galaxy.

Looking south

Located in the mid-heavens is one of the most magnificent of all constellations, Orion. As we saw earlier, it is an excellent celestial signpost. It helps us locate the brightest star in the sky, Sirius, in Canis Major, and other bright stars in nearby constellations. Among them, the star Aldebaran, the eye of Taurus, is noticeably red in color, as is Betelgeuse in Orion itself.

24

▶ These two views of the winter sky show the constellations observers will see looking north (top) and south (bottom) at about 11 p.m. during the first week in January every year. To identify the constellations, look at the list on page 20. The exact position of the constellations in the sky vary according to the latitude. This means for example, that observers in the southern United States, looking south, will find the constellations a little higher in the sky than this map shows. Observers in the northern United States and Canada will find the constellations a little lower in the sky.

PHILIPS' PLANISPHERE
SHOWING THE
PRINCIPAL STARS
VISIBLE FOR EVERY HOUR
IN THE YEAR

The handy planisphere

A planisphere is a useful device for identifying the stars in the sky. It shows the constellations visible at any time of the night on any night of the year.

It is made up of two disks. The top one rotates over the bottom one. The bottom one has a map of the stars. The top one has a window. They both have scales around the edge. The top one has a scale marked in hours; the bottom one has a scale marked in days of the year. To find the stars visible for a particular time and on a particular date, you rotate the top disk until time and date line up. The window then reveals what constellations are visible in the heavens at that time.

Milky Way

Winter – looking North

Galaxy

E

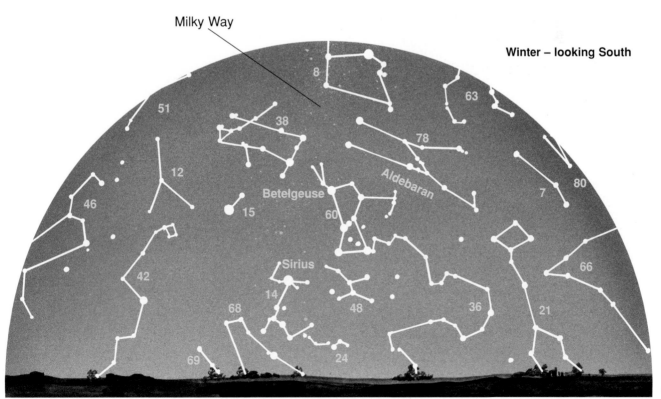

Milky Way

Winter – looking South

Betelgeuse

Aldebaran

Sirius

W

Summer stars

Looking north

You can see only a few changes in the constellations in the northern sky between winter and summer, but they now lie in opposite directions in the sky. The Big Dipper lies toward the west, and Cygnus is high up in the east, for example. You will now be able to see the whole of Cygnus and easily imagine it to be the outline of a flying swan, with neck outstretched.

Looking south

The bright star almost directly overhead is Vega, in the constellation Lyra. It forms a noticeable triangle with two other bright stars farther east. They are Deneb in Cygnus and Altair in Aquila. These three stars are a feature of summer skies and form what is called the Summer Triangle.

Low down near the horizon is a collection of very bright stars in the constellations Sagittarius and Scorpius. Observers in the southern United States should be able to see the whole of Scorpius, a well-named constellation depicting a scorpion with its curved tail and deadly sting.

▶These two views of the summer sky show the constellations observers will see looking north (top) and south (bottom) at about 11 p.m. during the first week in July every year. The exact positions of the constellations in the sky vary according to latitude. This means for example, that observers in the southern United States, looking south, will find the constellations a little higher in the sky than this map shows. Observers in the northern United States and Canada will find the constellations a little lower in the sky. To identify the constellations, look at the list on page 20.

26

Going to a planetarium is a good introduction to the starry heavens. A complicated projector throws an image of the night sky onto a domed ceiling. It can project a view of the sky as it would appear to an observer on any part of the Earth and for any time of the year.

Summer – looking North

Milky Way

40

9

34

31

25

13

84

20

45

62

83

18

Galaxy

11

63

1

8

80

86

46

51

66

E

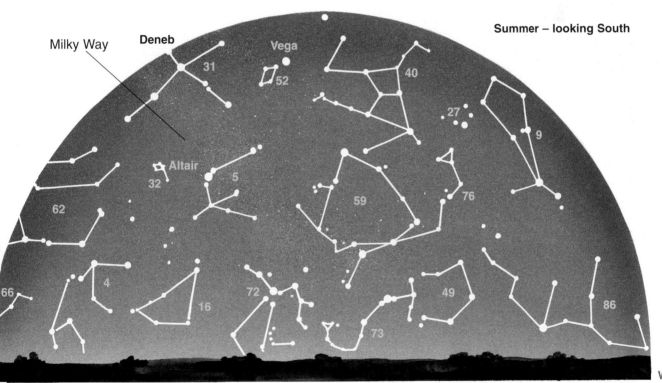

Summer – looking South

Milky Way

Deneb

Vega

31

52

40

27

9

32

Altair

5

76

62

59

66

4

16

72

49

86

73

W

2

What Stars Are Like

◀ This is a beautiful open cluster of stars in the far southern constellation Crux, the Southern Cross. It is often called the Jewel Box because the stars sparkle like precious jewels.

When you look up at the night sky, the stars appear as tiny points of light. Even when you look at them through a telescope, they don't appear any bigger, but if you could travel through space to see them close up, you would find that they are enormous.

Stars are great globes of searing hot gas, which give out energy as light, heat, and other radiation. They look tiny in the night sky only because they lie so very far away. Distances to the stars are measured in many millions of millions of miles. Strictly, we should say that all the stars except one lie very far away. There is one star that is on our celestial doorstep. It is the star we know as the Sun.

In this chapter, we look at what the Sun and the other stars are like. We find that many stars travel through space with companions. We also look at the great billowing clouds of matter that exists between the stars. It is in such clouds that stars are born.

▶This night sky view shows a region in the constellation Cygnus, the Swan. The bright star at the center is called Deneb. It is the brightest star in Cygnus and the 19th brightest in the whole heavens. It is much farther away than the other bright stars - at a distance of more than 1,600 light-years.

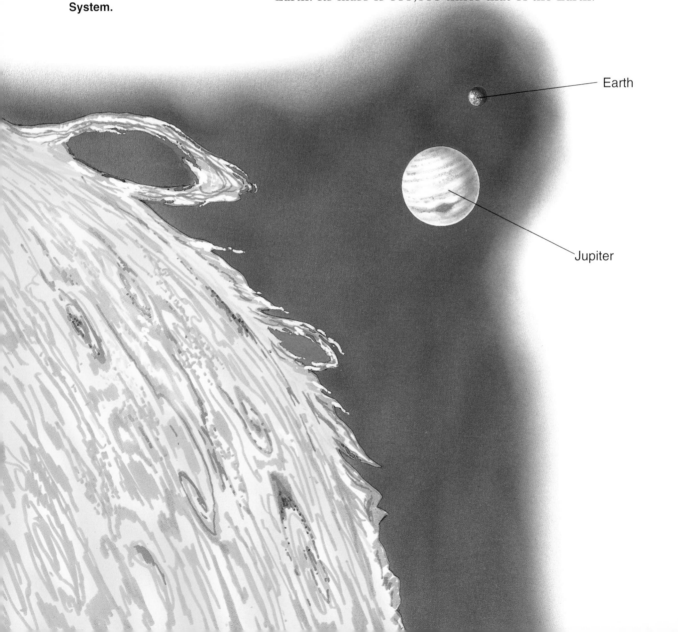

Our local star

The star we call the Sun breathes life into the Earth. Without the Sun's warmth and light, the world would be dead. Plants and animals would not be able to live.

Q It is easy to understand why living things need warmth, but why is light so essential to life on Earth?

Average star

The Sun is a very ordinary kind of star, not particularly big nor particularly bright. It measures about 865,000 miles (1,400,000 km) in diameter, so it is much bigger than the Earth. Its mass is 333,000 times that of the Earth.

30

▼ The Sun dwarfs not only the Earth, but also Jupiter, the largest planet in the Solar System.

Earth

Jupiter

The Earth is one of nine bodies that circle around the Sun in space. We call these bodies the planets. Going out from the Sun, the planets are Mercury, Venus, Earth, Mars, Jupiter, Saturn, Uranus, Neptune, and Pluto. The Sun's family, or solar system, also includes smaller bodies such as the asteroids, along with still smaller ones, such as comets and meteors.

Nuclear energy

The Sun is about 93 million miles (150 million km) away from Earth, but we can still feel its great heat. This heat is only a tiny fraction of the energy the Sun pours into space.

The surface of the Sun has a temperature of about 10,000°F (5,500°C), but it is much hotter inside. In the center, the temperature reaches more than 27,000,000°F (15,000,000°C). At this temperature the main gas in the Sun, hydrogen, becomes fuel in the process that produces the Sun's energy. It is a process that involves the fusing, or combining together, of the nuclei (centers) of the hydrogen atoms (see diagram).

31

▼ Nuclear fusion produces the energy that keeps the Sun shining. In the process, the nuclei of four hydrogen atoms come together to form the nucleus of a helium atom, and huge amounts of energy are released as radiation. This radiation includes invisible gamma rays, X-rays, and radio waves, as well as light rays we can see and heat rays we can feel.

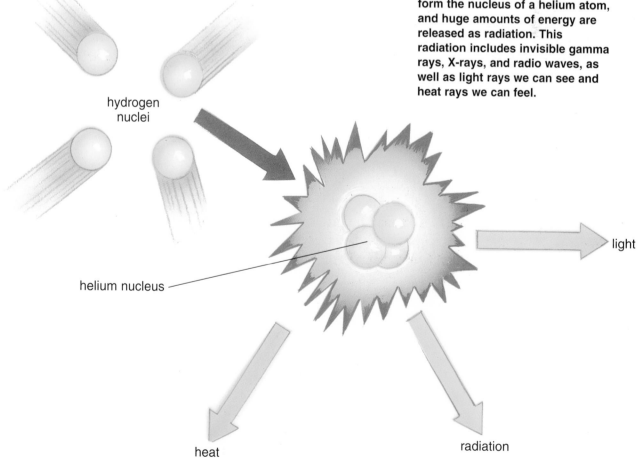

hydrogen nuclei

helium nucleus

light

heat

radiation

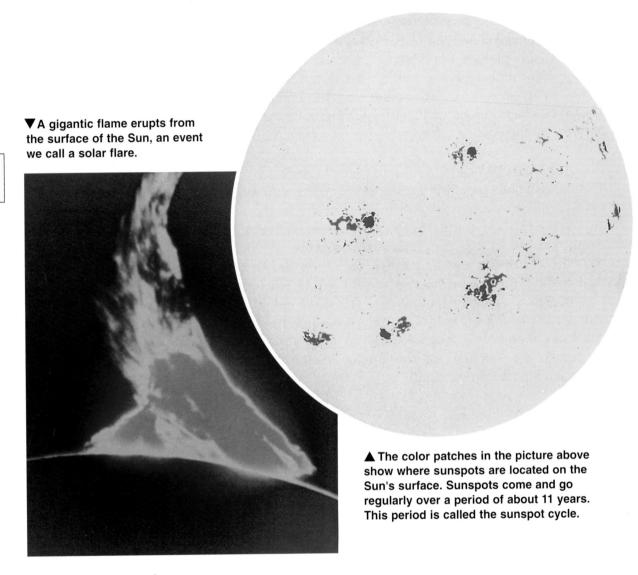

▼A gigantic flame erupts from the surface of the Sun, an event we call a solar flare.

▲ The color patches in the picture above show where sunspots are located on the Sun's surface. Sunspots come and go regularly over a period of about 11 years. This period is called the sunspot cycle.

The Sun's surface

The surface of the Sun is a bubbling, boiling mass of flaming gas. We call this visible surface the photosphere ("light sphere"). Fiery tongues of gas called flares, and fountains of gas called prominences constantly shoot high above the surface. Cooler, darker patches called sunspots appear from time to time.

The Sun also gives off a constant stream of invisible particles. We call it the solar wind. When the solar wind reaches Earth, it can upset the atmosphere. This often gives rise to colored glows in far northern and far southern skies. We call these glows the aurora, or the northern and southern lights.

WORKOUT

Light travels at a speed of about 186,000 miles (300,000 km) a second. Work out (A) how far away from the Earth Proxima Centauri is, (B) how much farther away Proxima Centauri is than the Sun.

Stars near and far

Most of the stars we see in the night sky are a lot like the Sun, though they may differ from it in size, brightness, temperature, and color. They are all great globes of gas, made up mainly of hydrogen and helium. They produce their energy from nuclear fusion reactions in their hot interiors.

Distances to the stars

The distances to the stars are so great that they are difficult to imagine. Even the closest stars lie tens of millions of millions of miles away. The closest star to us lies in the constellation Centaurus and is called Proxima Centauri. It is so far away that its light takes about 4 years 3½ months to reach us. We can say that it is more than 4 light-years away.

Astronomers often measure distances to the stars in terms of light-years – the distance light travels in a year – rather than in miles or kilometers. It is a much more convenient unit.

33

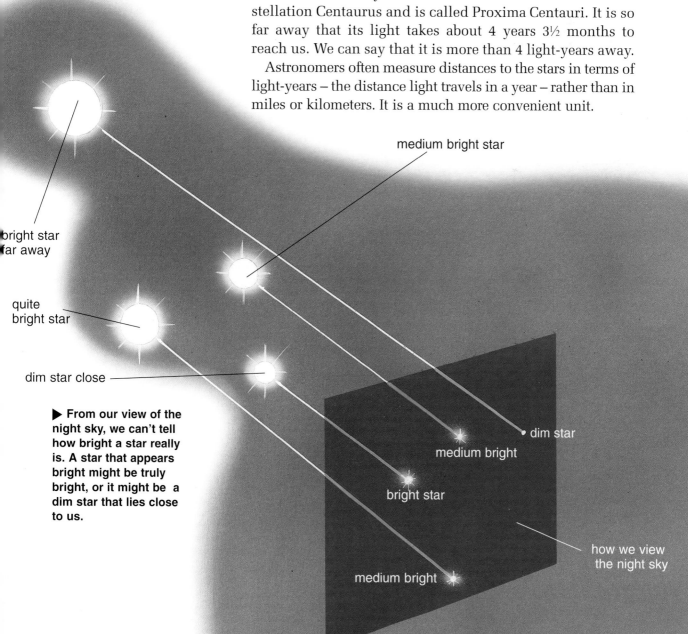

bright star far away

quite bright star

dim star close

medium bright star

medium bright

dim star

bright star

medium bright

how we view the night sky

▶ From our view of the night sky, we can't tell how bright a star really is. A star that appears bright might be truly bright, or it might be a dim star that lies close to us.

Star brightness

We use a scale of magnitudes to measure the brightness of stars. We grade the stars we can see with the naked eye into six classes of brightness. We say the brightest are of the first magnitude, and the faintest are of the sixth magnitude. On this scale, a star of one magnitude is about 2.5 times as bright as one of the next magnitude.

Q How much brighter is a first magnitude star compared with the faintest star we can see?

Measuring distances

As we saw earlier, the brightness of a star as we see it gives little indication of its true brightness. That depends on how far away the star is. This raises the question: how do we measure distances to the stars?

We can measure the distance to some of the nearer stars using simple geometry. We use what is called the parallax method. An object appears to move against a distant background when viewed from different positions.

In the diagram (right), we wish to measure the distance to nearby star S. To do this, we carefully measure the position of the star in the sky when the Earth is at point A in its orbit. We take another measurement of the star's position

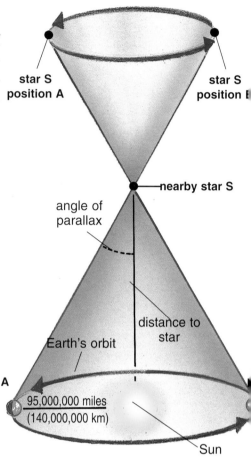

star S
position A

star S
position B

nearby star S

angle of
parallax

distance to
star

Earth's orbit

A

95,000,000 miles
(140,000,000 km)

Sun

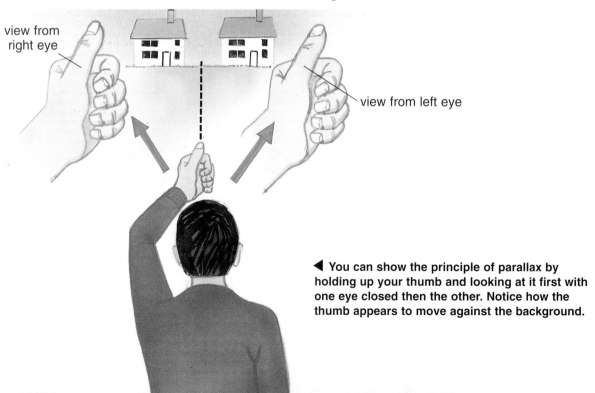

view from
right eye

view from left eye

◀ **You can show the principle of parallax by holding up your thumb and looking at it first with one eye closed then the other. Notice how the thumb appears to move against the background.**

when the Earth is at point B in its orbit. We now have enough information to calculate the star's distance. We have the star's change in position against the background of stars, and we know the distance from one side of the Earth's orbit to the other.

This method works only for a few hundred stars. The other stars are so far away that they show no parallax, or change in position.

WORKOUT

The Sun is an average sized star. Many stars are much smaller and many stars are much bigger. By measurement, figure out how much bigger large and giant stars are compared with the Sun, and how much bigger the Sun is than the other dwarf stars. This diagram gives a rough idea of star sizes.

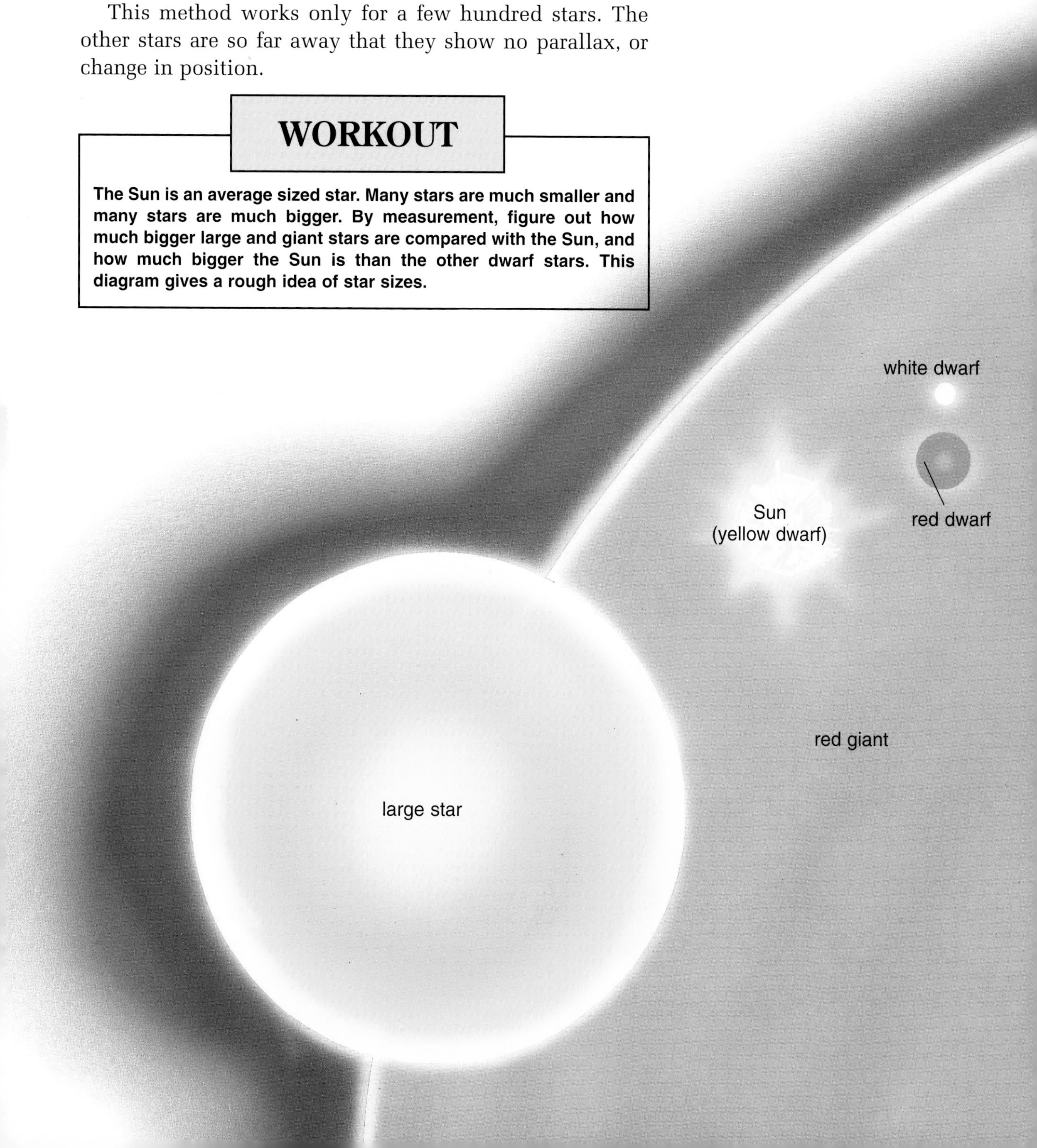

white dwarf

Sun
(yellow dwarf)

red dwarf

red giant

large star

Star companions

If you look carefully at the middle star in the handle of the Big Dipper, you can see another star close by. We call this combination a double star. The two stars look close together, but they are really far apart. They just happen to lie in the same direction in space.

Many pairs of stars in the heavens actually are close together. We call such a pair of stars a binary. Interestingly, out of every 100 stars, nearly 50 are binaries. Of the same 100 stars, about 30 travel through space by themselves, as our Sun does. The remaining twenty are multiple stars, made up of three or more stars traveling through space together.

In a binary and multiple star system, the stars are linked by gravity. They circle around one another, or rather, around a common center of gravity.

▶ In the diagram, stars 1 and 2 form a close binary system. A third star (3) circles around them farther out, making it a triple-star system. Often in such a system the stars are so close together that they appear as a single star, even through a telescope.

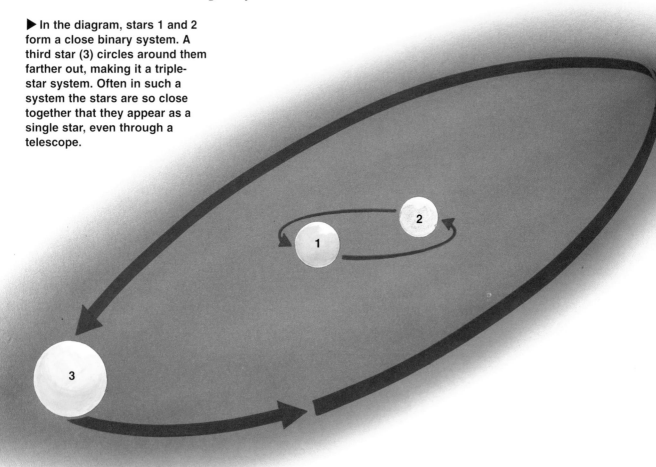

▶ This picture shows the most famous open star cluster in the heavens, the Pleiades, or Seven Sisters. All the stars were born at the same time and are relatively young. They are surrounded by nebulosity, or clouds of hot gas.

Star clusters

In some parts of the heavens, stars cluster together in larger groups. If you look at the constellation Taurus, you can see one such cluster easily (see the map at the bottom of page 25). It is the Pleiades, also called the Seven Sisters. It is so called because, if your eyes are good, you can see its seven brightest stars. All together, there are more than 150 stars in the group. They were all born at the same time and are traveling through space together.

The Pleiades is an example of what is called an open cluster. Its stars are relatively far apart. In another kind of cluster, however, stars are packed tightly together into a globe shape. This type is called a globular cluster.

WORKOUT

If you went stargazing in South America, you would easily see this globular cluster with the naked eye. It looks like a bright star in the constellation Centaurus and is called Omega Centauri. Astronomers think that it contains as many as one million stars packed tightly together. Assuming each star is the same size as the Sun, figure out how many Earths you would need to balance Omega Centauri on a pair of imaginary scales. (Use data given on page 30.)

Clouds among the stars

If you look at the constellation Orion, you can see a bright patch beneath the three stars that form Orion's belt. Through a telescope, you can see that the patch is a great glowing cloud. It is a fine example of what is called a nebula (the Latin word for cloud).

There are many such clouds in the heavens, occupying regions of space many light-years across. They are made up of a mixture of gas and fine dust.

The Orion nebula is an example of a bright nebula. It is lit up by stars embedded within it. Some nebulae, however, have no nearby stars to light them up. They remain dark. We can see them when they block the light of stars behind them.

Organic matter

The main gas in nebulae is hydrogen, and the dust consists mainly of grains of carbon. There are also traces of many other substances as well. They include water, ammonia, alcohol, formaldehyde, and several other organic compounds.

Q The presence of organic compounds scattered throughout space is interesting. Why?

IT'S AMAZING!

The density of the matter in a nebula is very low. The volume of a nebula the size of the Earth would weigh only a few pounds.

▶ **This beautiful nebula is called the Trifid because of the three dark dust lanes it contains. The Trifid is one of several outstanding nebulae in the constellation Sagittarius.**

▼ **We see bright nebulae in the heavens when stars within them or nearby make them glow. We see dark nebulae when gas clouds are not lit up and blot out the light of distant stars.**

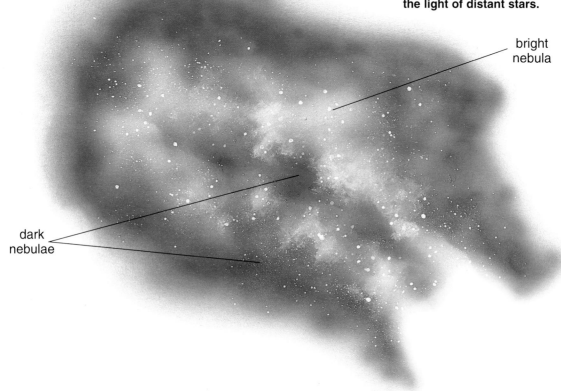

bright nebula

dark nebulae

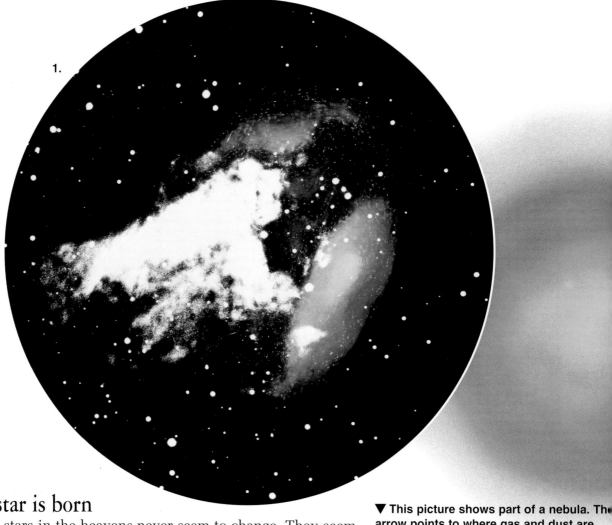

1.

A star is born

The stars in the heavens never seem to change. They seem to shine steadily, year by year and century by century. But stars do change. Eventually, all the stars we see will die and fade away. New stars will appear to take their place, and they too will die and fade away in turn.

This process will take a very long time because the life of a typical star is measured in billions of years. The Sun, for example, is already five billion years old, and it should keep on shining as it does today for another five billion years.

Stars are born in nebulae, the great clouds of gas and dust that exist in space. They start to form when part of a nebula begins to condense, or collapse. The matter in the cloud gets denser and denser as the collapse continues. It starts to form a roughly spherical mass.

▼ This picture shows part of a nebula. The arrow points to where gas and dust are condensing to form a denser mass. In milli of years, this mass will become a star.

As the particles of matter fall into this mass, they pick up energy, just as a ball picks up energy when you let it drop.

Q The same force is at work in both cases. What force is it?

Lighting the furnace

As the particles join the spherical mass, they give up their energy, which reappears as heat. The more the mass collapses, the hotter it becomes. As its temperature rises, it starts to glow. In time, the temperature at the heart of the mass reaches many millions of degrees. This is high enough to trigger off nuclear reactions between hydrogen atoms (see page 31). The mass of matter becomes a star and begins shining steadily.

It takes a star like the Sun about 50 million years to reach this stage from the time the gas cloud started to condense.

2.

3.

Stages in the birth of a star.

(1) A huge nebula of gas and dust measuring many light-years across begins to shrink.

(2) As it shrinks, it heats up. As the temperature of the shrinking mass rises, it becomes visible, glowing first a dull red, then orange, then yellow.

(3) By the time it has shrunk to less than a million miles across, it is so hot that nuclear reactions begin inside it. It becomes hotter still and starts to shine as a star.

A star dies

Once nuclear reactions start up inside it, a star like the Sun will keep on shining steadily for about 10 billion years. Then it will start to run out of hydrogen, the "fuel" for the nuclear reactions. Other nuclear reactions then take place, which cause the star to heat up and expand greatly in size and glow red. It becomes a class of star called a red giant.

A red giant in time runs out of fuel too, and gradually shrinks. As it shrinks, it heats up and becomes whiter. After many millions of years, it turns into a dense body called a white dwarf.

A star with a much greater mass than the Sun has a much shorter life. It reaches the red giant stage after perhaps only a few million years. Then it keeps on expanding until it becomes a supergiant, several times bigger still. Then it blasts itself apart in a mighty explosion, which we call a supernova.

What remains of the star then collapses. It may then form a tiny body called a neutron star. Such a star is made up of atomic particles called neutrons, packed closely together. It is much denser, even, than a white dwarf.

42

WORKOUT

A typical white dwarf is only about as big as the Earth, yet it has about the same mass as the Sun. Using data on page 30, how much denser is the matter in a white dwarf than the matter the Earth is made of?
If the average density of Earth matter is about 3 ounces per cubic inch (5.5 grams per cc), how much would 1 cubic inch (1 cc) of white dwarf matter weigh?

red giant

WORKOUT

Astronomers believe that the Sun will expand into a red giant with 30 times its present diameter. Calculate the volume of the red giant Sun. How many present-day Suns would fit into the red giant Sun?

A much larger star dies a more dramatic death. It expands until it becomes an enormous supergiant. Then it explodes spectacularly, ending up as a neutron star or a black hole.

supergiant

The collapsing star may continue collapsing beyond the neutron star stage and form a black hole. This is a region of space with enormous gravity. Nothing can escape from its incredibly strong gravitational pull, not even light. This is why we call it a black hole.

◀ The way a star dies depends upon how massive it is. A star like the Sun gradually expands into a red giant, then gradually shrinks again until it becomes a white dwarf.

white dwarf

Studying the stars

Astronomy had its beginnings thousands of years ago when the early priest-astrologers began their careful observations of the heavens. Until nearly four centuries ago, astronomers had to rely on their eyes alone for observation. Then in the early 1600s, the Italian scientist Galileo ushered in a revolution. He built the first practical telescope and trained it on the heavens. The telescope has remained the astronomer's most important instrument ever since.

The refractor

Galileo built his telescope using glass lenses. It was a type we call a refractor, because lenses refract (bend) light that passes through them. A refractor has two lenses (see diagram below). The larger one at the far end of the telescope is called the objective. It forms an image of a distant object. You look through a smaller lens, called the eyepiece, which magnifies the image.

▲ A view of one of the finest observatories in the world. It is the Kitt Peak National Observatory in Arizona. The domes house the telescopes. At night, shutters open to expose the telescopes to the night sky.

The reflector

The British scientist Isaac Newton built another type of telescope in the 1660s. It is a type we call a reflector, because it uses reflecting mirrors to gather light.

Newton's design is still popular, and is called the Newtonian. It uses a large curved mirror (the primary) at the bottom of the telescope tube to collect incoming light. This mirror then reflects the light onto a flat mirror (the secondary) further up the tube. This second mirror reflects an image into an eyepiece set in the side of the tube.

All of the large telescopes professional astronomers use are reflectors.

IT'S AMAZING!

Some modern telescopes are so sensitive to light that they would be able to detect the light from a burning candle 15,000 miles (25,000 km) away.

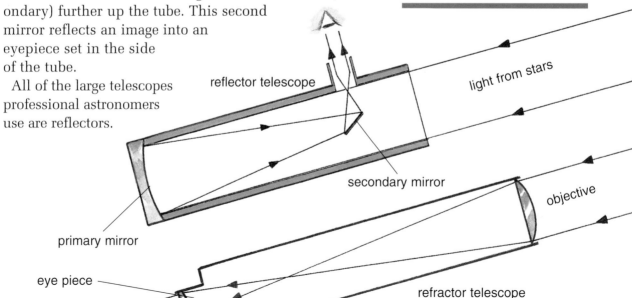

reflector telescope

light from stars

secondary mirror

primary mirror

objective

eye piece

refractor telescope

BUILD A TELESCOPE

You can build a refracting telescope yourself quite easily. You will need to buy two suitable lenses from a scientific supplier for the objective and the eyepiece. (You can get catalogs for such lenses from Edmund Scientific, in Barrington, N.J.) For the objective, you need a lens with a focal length of about 20 inches (50 cm). For the eyepiece, you need a lens with a short focal length, say 1¼ in (3 cm).

You can make the telescope tubes by (1) rolling up sheets of black cardboard. The tube that will house the eyepiece must be able to slide into the objective tube. (2) Fasten the lenses in the tubes with a suitable glue.

Train your telescope on a distant object and slide the eyepiece tube in or out until you get the object in focus. (You may need to experiment with the lengths of the tubes to get a satisfactory result.) When you are happy with your telescope, train it on the heavens and see what you can see. Look at the stars, the Milky Way, and the Moon. Watch for meteors and comets.

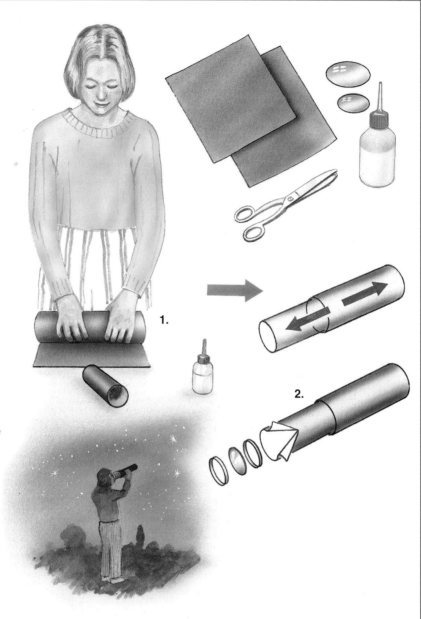

1.

2.

45

<u>NEVER</u> TRY TO LOOK AT THE SUN WITH YOUR TELESCOPE – IT CAN BLIND YOU.

Long-distance information

Stars lie millions upon millions of miles away from us, yet astronomers can tell us a lot about them. They can tell us how hot they are, what they are made of, how fast they are moving, and many other things besides.

How can they do this? Incredibly, they can get this information by examining the faint rays of light that reach us from the stars. To the naked eye, the light from one star looks much like the light from another, but instruments can show the differences between the light from different stars.

One of the main instruments astronomers use to examine starlight is the spectroscope. This instrument splits up the light into a spectrum, or spread of color. It is from the spectrum that astronomers learn so much about a star.

The picture below shows the spectrum of a typical star. You notice it is crossed by dark lines. From the positions of these lines, astronomers can tell what chemical elements are present in the star. They can also tell whether the star is moving toward or away from us. By measuring the energy in different parts of the spectrum, astronomers can estimate the temperature of the star.

Viewing from space

Stars give out all kinds of other rays besides light. If we can study these rays, such as gamma rays and X-rays, we will learn much more about what stars are like. The problem is that most of these rays are blocked by the Earth's atmosphere. However, we can now send instruments into space on satellites to study these rays. Astronomy satellites are also sent into space carrying ordinary light telescopes. The Hubble Space Telescope is an example. It has been sending back excellent pictures of stars and galaxies since it was repaired in orbit in 1993.

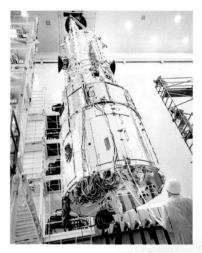

▲ The Hubble telescope is large and heavy. It measures 42 feet (13 meters) long and weighs 12 tons (11 tonnes). It gathers the light from heavenly bodies with a main mirror 95 inches (2.4 meters) across.

light

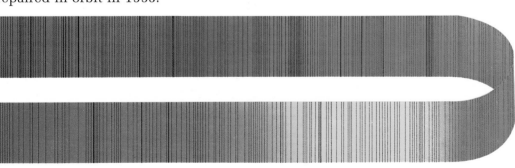

The spectrum of a typical star is crosse[d] by dark lines. Astronomers can ga[in] an amazing amount [of] information by studying the position[s] of these spectral line[s]

46

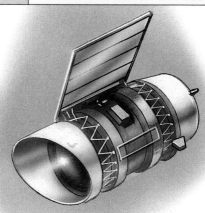

▶ This space satellite is named IRAS. It was launched in the early 1980s and peered at the Universe with infrared eyes. It spotted regions of space where stars were being born.

47

▼ Stars give out energy in many different forms – as light and as invisible radiation, including radio waves.

radiation

radio waves

Stars also send out radio waves, and these can pass through the atmosphere. This has led to the science of radio astronomy. Radio astronomers "tune in" to stars and galaxies with radio telescopes. They are huge metal dishes. The biggest dish has a diameter 1,000 feet (305 meters) across. It is built into a mountaintop near Arecibo on the Caribbean island of Puerto Rico.

This is a radio image of a distant galaxy. It was produced by a computer from radio waves the galaxy is sending out.

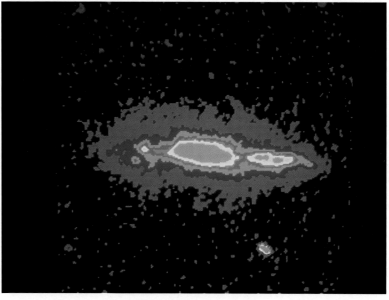

3

A Universe of Galaxies

◄ The best known of the outer galaxies, the Andromeda galaxy. It is a spiral galaxy similar to our own galaxy, but it is much bigger. It is one of about 30 galaxies that lie relatively close to us in space.

When you look at the night sky, you can see stars in all directions. They seem to be scattered throughout space. Is the Universe like this – a vast expanse of space sprinkled with stars? The answer is no.

If we could travel many thousands of light-years out into space and look back, we would see that all the stars in our galaxy are in fact grouped together. They form a great star island floating in space. From our distant vantage point we would see other star islands as well.

Stars throughout the Universe are gathered into such islands, which we call galaxies. There are billions of stars in each galaxy, and there are billions of galaxies in the Universe.

In this chapter, we look at our own galaxy and at some of the others that occupy the Universe. We look back 15,000 million years to when the Universe began and speculate on how it might end.

▶ Part of the neighboring galaxy we call the Large Magellanic Cloud. People in the far Southern Hemisphere can see this galaxy with the naked eye.

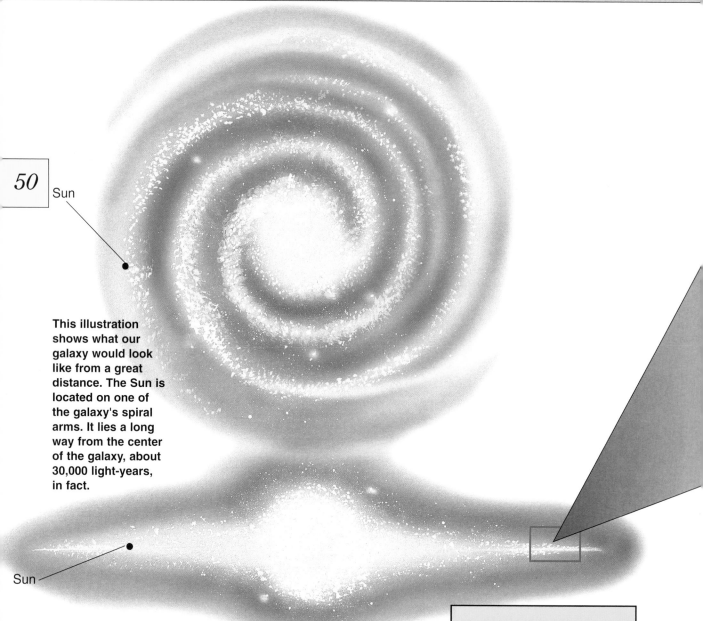

50

Sun

This illustration shows what our galaxy would look like from a great distance. The Sun is located on one of the galaxy's spiral arms. It lies a long way from the center of the galaxy, about 30,000 light-years, in fact.

Sun

Our galaxy

On a really dark night, you can see a faint band of light arching across the sky. We call it the Milky Way. In northern skies, it passes through the constellations Cassiopeia and Cygnus, for example, and through Aquila, Sagittarius, and Scorpius farther south. (The position of the Milky Way is marked on the star maps shown on pages 25 and 27.)

Our galaxy is roughly disk-shaped, with a bulge in the middle. It is huge, measuring something like 100,000 light-years

WORKOUT

It takes the Sun about 225 million years to journey once around the center of the galaxy. How far does it travel during this time? Give your answer in light-years. How many journeys has the Sun made around the center of the galaxy?

▲ A region of the Milky Way in Sagittarius, packed with stars and nebulae. The Milky Way is dense and bright here because the center of the galaxy lies in this direction.

▶ Our galaxy would look much like this when viewed from afar. This is a similar kind of galaxy found in far southern skies.

across. Most of the stars in the galaxy are located on arms that curve away from the center. Astronomers estimate that there must be at least 100,000 million stars in the Milky Way Galaxy all together.

Like most bodies in space, the galaxy rotates. Viewed from a great distance, it would look like a flaming pinwheel.

The outer galaxies

Our galaxy is just one of billions that populate the Universe. Many of the other galaxies are of the same type. They are spiral galaxies, in which the stars are located on curved arms. These galaxies have much the same mix of stars, clusters, and nebulae as our own galaxy.

We can see a nearby spiral galaxy with the naked eye in the constellation Andromeda. The Andromeda galaxy (see page 48) is about half again as big as our own galaxy and lies more than two million light-years away.

A number of smaller galaxies are much closer. The two closest are the Large and Small Magellanic Clouds, which can be seen in far southern skies. The Large Magellanic Cloud lies only 170,000 light-years away. It is a rather shapeless mass, and astronomers class it as an irregular galaxy.

Active galaxies

Galaxies give out an enormous amount of energy because of the billions of stars they contain. Some exceptional galaxies give out more energy than usual. Sometimes they give out this energy as ordinary light and sometimes as other radiation, such as radio waves.

We call galaxies with an exceptional energy output active galaxies. Astronomers think that black holes might be the source of this energy.

▶ Most of the galaxies we see in the sky have these kinds of shapes. Some are spherical or oval in shape: we call them ellipticals. Some are spirals, like our own galaxy. The arms may be close together or far apart. Others have a spiral form but have a bar running through the central bulge: we call them barred-spiral galaxies.

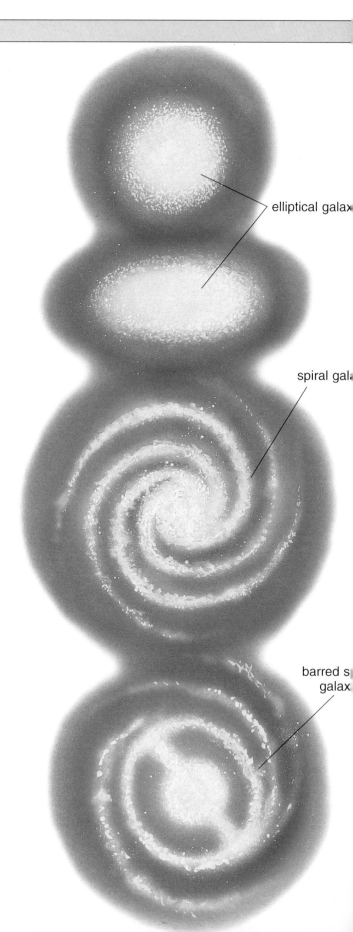

elliptical galax

spiral gal

barred s
galax

52

IT'S AMAZING!

Among the most baffling heavenly bodies astronomers know are quasars. They look like stars, but are tens of thousands of times farther away. To be visible from such a distance, they must be incredibly bright. In fact, astronomers believe that they have the energy output of hundreds of galaxies put together.

▲ The Large Magellanic Cloud, the nearest galaxy to our own. It is one of a group of about 30 nearby galaxies, called the Local Group.

◀ This is one of the most distinctive galaxies in the heavens. It is aptly called the Whirlpool. It is actually two galaxies connected together.

The expanding Universe

Astronomers can find out whether a star is moving toward or away from us by examining the spectrum of the light it gives out (see page 46). They can find out whether a galaxy is moving toward or away from us in the same way. When they look at the spectra of light given out by galaxies, they find that all the outer galaxies are rushing away from us. And the farther the galaxies are away, the faster they appear to be traveling.

It seems as if the whole Universe is expanding, as if from some kind of explosion. Astronomers now believe that this is true. They reckon that, about 15 billion years ago, a gigantic explosion created the Universe and set it expanding. They call this event the Big Bang.

How will it end?

Most astronomers agree that the Universe began in a Big Bang, but they are not so sure about how it will end. Some think that the Universe will carry on expanding as it is today for many billions of years to come until it runs out of energy. This idea is called the open Universe.

Other astronomers think that the gravity of all the matter in the Universe will one day stop it expanding. This is the idea of the closed Universe. Gravity will in time start to pull back the galaxies. The Universe will start to shrink. Eventually, all the matter will be concentrated together in an event often called the Big Crunch. This will signal the end of the Universe. But it could also trigger off another Big Bang and create a new Universe.

▶ A Big Bang created the Universe. The newborn Universe was fantastically hot and filled with radiation. Matter began to form as the Universe expanded and gradually cooled down. No one knows when this matter began condensing into stars and galaxies. But we know that it must have happened when the Universe was just a few billion years old.

▶ This pictures a part of the Universe as it is today. It is a photograph showing part of a distant cluster of galaxies. The Universe is made up of many such clusters, which may each contain up to thousands of galaxies.

Milestones

ABOUT 3000 BC Sumerian and Babylonian stargazers in the Middle East began recording their observations of the stars.

2000 BC The Greek astronomer Hipparchus compiled the first major star catalog, listing more than 1,000 stars.

AD 1054 Chinese astronomers reported a new star in Taurus – it was the supernova that spawned the famous Crab nebula.

1609/10 The Italian scientist Galileo first trained a telescope on the heavens, ushering in a revolution in observational astronomy.

1660s The English scientist Isaac Newton built the first reflecting telescope.

1781 Charles Messier in France published a catalog of nebulae and star clusters. Many such bodies are now known by their Messier (M) numbers.

1838 The German astronomer Friedrich Wilhelm Bessel determined the first accurate distance to a star (known as 61 Cygni) using the principle of parallax.

1888 The Danish astronomer Johan Ludwig Emil Dreyer compiled the New General Catalog (NGC) of Clusters and Nebulae. Most clusters and galaxies are now known by their NGC numbers.

1912 US astronomer Henrietta Leavitt discovered the relationship between the period of variation in brightness and the true brightness of Cepheid stars. This became a valuable yardstick for estimating distances in space

1918 The 100-inch (2.5-meter) Hooker telescope was completed on Mt Wilson, near Los Angeles. It was the first giant telescope.

1925 Working with the Hooker telescope, the US astronomer Edwin Hubble confirmed that certain nebulae were really other galaxies.

1937 US engineer Grote Reber built the first radio telescope to tune into radio waves from outer space, so founding radio astronomy.

1948 The 200-inch (5-meter) telescope was built on Mt Palomar, near Los Angeles. It was named after US astronomer George Ellery Hale.

1963 US astronomer Maarten Schmidt reported the extraordinary distance of the star-like body 3C273, which became recognized as the first quasar.

1978 US satellite Einstein Observatory discovered a large number of X-ray sources in the heavens.

1983 US satellite IRAS scanned the heavens at infrared wavelengths. It spotted regions where stars were being born and detected other possible solar systems.

1987 The brightest supernova this century erupted in a nearby galaxy, the Large Magellanic Cloud. It was visible to the naked eye.

1990 The Hubble Space Telescope was launched. After in-orbiting repairs three years later, it began producing the best-ever images of the heavens.

1992 Data returned by US satellite COBE seemed to confirm the Big-Bang theory of the origin of the Universe.

Glossary

AURORA A colorful glow seen in far northern and far southern skies, produced when charged particles from the Sun collide with air particles in the upper atmosphere.

BIG BANG An event that is thought to have created the Universe, some 15,000 million years ago.

BINARY A double star in which two relatively close stars revolve around each other.

BLACK HOLE A body whose gravity is so intense that not even light can escape from it.

BRIGHTNESS See **MAGNITUDE**.

CELESTIAL SPHERE An imaginary sphere around the Earth to which the stars seem to be fixed.

CONSTELLATIONS Imaginary patterns the bright stars make in the heavens.

DOUBLE STAR A pair of stars that appear close together in the heavens.

ECLIPTIC The apparent path the Sun takes each year around the celestial sphere.

GALAXY An "island" of stars in space. Galaxies are usually elliptical or spiral in shape. The spiral galaxy to which our Sun belongs is known as the Milky Way.

GLOBULAR CLUSTER A group of hundreds of thousands of stars, clustered together into a globe shape. Several hundred clusters circle around the centers of galaxies.

GRAVITY The force with which the Earth attracts any object on it or near it in space. The other heavenly bodies exert a similar force. Gravity is one of the great forces of the Universe; it literally holds the Universe together.

HYDROGEN The simplest of all the chemical elements and also the most plentiful element in the Universe.

INTERSTELLAR Between the stars.

INTERSTELLAR MATTER Gas and dust found in the space between the stars.

LIGHT-YEAR A common unit for measuring distances in astronomy, being the distance light travels in a year. 1 light-year is about 6 trillion miles (9.5 trillion km).

MAGNITUDE A scale on which the brightness of stars is measured. The brightest stars in the sky are of the 1st magnitude; the dimmest ones are of the 6th magnitude.

MILKY WAY A diffuse band of light that spans the heavens. It represents a cross-section of the Milky Way galaxy.

NEBULA (plural NEBULAE) A cloud of dust and gas in between the stars. It may be bright or dark, depending on whether it is lit up or not.

NEUTRON STAR An incredibly dense star made up of the atomic particles, neutrons.

NUCLEAR FUSION The process by which the Sun and the stars produce their energy. It is a process in which the nuclei (centers) of hydrogen atoms fuse (combine) together. When this happens, enormous energy is released as light, heat, and other radiation.

PARALLAX The apparent shift of a nearby object against a distant background when viewed from a

58

different angle. This principle is used to measure the distance to some nearby stars.

PLANETS Large bodies that circle in space around the Sun. The Earth is a planet. There are eight others, some much smaller, and some much bigger than the Earth. Other stars almost certainly have planets circling around them.

POLE STAR A bright star that lies in the heavens close to the northern celestial pole. It is also known as the North Star, but astronomers call it Polaris. There is no convenient pole star in the southern celestial hemisphere.

PROMINENCE A fountain of gas that shoots high above the surface of the Sun. We can see prominences only during a total eclipse of the Sun.

PULSAR A neutron star that emits rapid pulses of radiation as it rotates.

QUASAR A very remote heavenly body that looks like a star but has the energy output of hundreds of galaxies. "Quasar" is short for "quasi-stellar object".

RADIATION Rays, such as those given off by the Sun and the stars, including light rays, X-rays, ultraviolet rays, infrared rays, and radio waves. These rays are all different kinds of electromagnetic radiation.

RADIO ASTRONOMY The branch of astronomy that studies heavenly bodies by the radio waves they give out.

RED GIANT A large red star that represents a late stage in the life of a star like the Sun.

SOLAR SYSTEM The family of the Sun, which travels through space as a unit. It has the Sun at its center, and around the Sun circle nine planets (including the Earth), the asteroids, and many comets.

SOLAR WIND A stream of charged atomic particles given off by the Sun.

SPECTROSCOPE An instrument used to study the spectrum of starlight.

SPECTRUM A spread of color obtained by passing starlight through a spectroscope. It represents the different wavelengths in the starlight.

STAR A gaseous body that produces its own energy by nuclear fusion. It releases this energy as light, heat, and other radiation.

STELLAR Relating to the stars.

SUNSPOT An area of the Sun's surface that is darker and cooler than its surroundings. Sunspots come and go regularly over a period of about 11 years – the sunspot cycle.

SUPERGIANT A very large star, typically several hundred times larger in diameter than the Sun.

UNIVERSE Everything that exists: the Earth, the Sun, the Moon, the stars, galaxies, quasars, and even space itself.

WHITE DWARF A small, hot, and very dense body, which represents a late stage in the life of a star like the Sun.

ZODIAC An imaginary band in the heavens in which the Sun, the Moon, and the planets are always found. It is occupied by 12 constellations - the constellations of the zodiac. They are Aries, Pisces, Aquarius, Capricornus, Sagittarius, Scorpius, Libra, Virgo, Leo, Cancer, Gemini, and Taurus.

For Further Reading

Estallela, Robert.
Our Satellite: The Moon.
Barron, Hauppauge. 19894

George, Michael.
Stars.
Creative Education, Mankato. 1992.

Gustafson, John.
Stars, Clusters, and Galaxies.
Simon and Schuster, New York. 1993.

Henbest, Nigel.
The Night Sky.
EDC, Tulsa. 1993.

Mayes, S.
Why is Night Dark?
EDC, Tulsa. 1990.

Schatz, Dennis.
Astronomy Activity Book.
Simon and Schuster, New York. 1991.

Schultz, Ron.
Looking Inside Telescopes and the Night Sky.
John Muir, Santa Fe. 1995.

Souza, Dorothy.
Northern Lights: Nature in Action.
Carolrhoda Books, Minneapolis. 1993.

Stott, Carole.
Night Sky.
Dorling Kindersley, New York. 1994.

Wilson, David.
Star Track.
Lorien House, Black Mountain. 1994.

Answers

Page 11
Investigate
Join the dots. What animals did you manage to draw? Here are the two constellations, as imagined by ancient astronomers. They are Leo, the Lion; and Scorpius, the Scorpion.

clockwise. The top diagram shows the path of the stars around the southern celestial pole. They appear to circle clockwise.

2. If you stood at the North Pole and looked east – or indeed in any other direction, the stars would appear to travel parallel with the horizon from left to right.

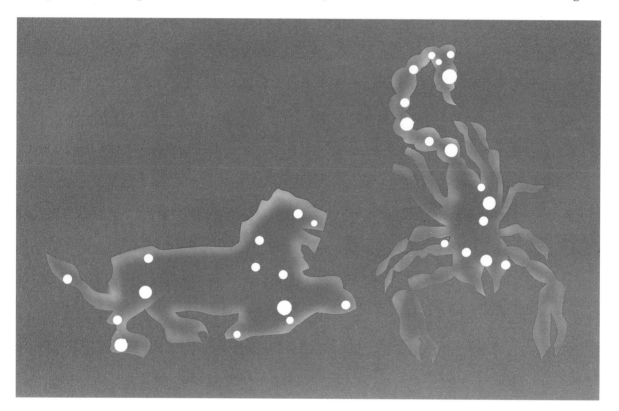

Page 14
The most noticeable effect of the Earth spinning on its axis is that it creates day and night. Day is when the part of the Earth you are on is facing toward the Sun. Night is when the part of the Earth you are on is facing away from the Sun.

Page 15
1. The bottom diagram shows the path of the stars around the northern celestial pole. They appear to circle counter-

3. If you stood on the Equator and looked east, the stars appear to travel vertically upward. If you looked west, they would appear to travel vertically downward.

Page 1
Observation
The sketch opposite shows the positions of the Big Dipper in the sky at about 11 pm for mid-March (spring), mid-June (summer), mid September (fall), and mid-December (winter).

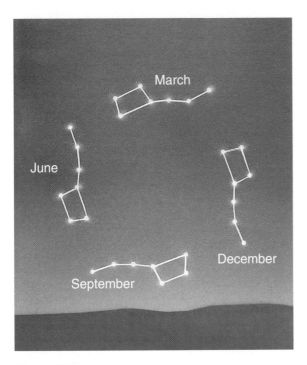

Page 17
You can't photograph the heavens for 24 hours at a time because for about half of this time it is daylight!

Page 18
The best-known star in the diagram is Sirius, because it is the brightest star in the heavens. It is often called the Dog Star because it is in the constellation Canis Major, the Great Dog.

Page 19
If I lived at the Equator, I would during the year see ALL of the constellations of the northern hemisphere and ALL of the constellations of the southern hemisphere.

Page 22
From the Earth, the Sun appears to travel through the heavens because the Earth is traveling round the Sun. So it takes the Sun one year to make a full circle of the heavens.

Page 30
Plants need the light from the Sun to make their food, in a process called photosynthesis ("making with light"). Animals can't make their own food. They must eat plants or eat other animals that eat plants. Hence, without light there would be no plants, and without plants there would be no life.

Page 33
Workout
1. The nearest star, Proxima Centauri, lies about 25 trillion miles from Earth, that is, 25 followed by 12 zeros.
2. Proxima Centauri is about 26,900 times farther away from the Earth than is the Sun.

Page 34
A first magnitude star is about 100 times (98 times as calculated) brighter than the faintest star we can see – a sixth magnitude star. (So a first magnitude star is about 2.5 cubed times brighter than a sixth magnitude star.)

Page 35
Workout
Measuring the stars in the diagram, the large star is about 4 times, and the supergiant star about 15 times larger in diameter then the Sun. In turn, the Sun has about twice the diameter of the red dwarf and about 5 times the diameter of the white dwarf.

Page 37
Workout
You would need 333 billion Earths to balance Omega Centauri on a pair of scales.

Page 38
Living things are made up of different

kinds of organic compounds. So the presence of organic compounds in space might suggest that life is common in the Universe. But astronomers have not yet found any evidence of other life forms in space.

Page 41

The force of gravity is at work both when you drop a ball and when particles of matter fall into the gathering mass of gas and dust formed when a star is being born.

Page 42
Workout

1. The volume of the red giant Sun in cubic miles would be about 9 billion trillion, that is, 9 followed by 21 zeros. (In cubic kilometers, the volume would be about 36 billion trillion.)

2. The density of a white dwarf is 333,000 times the density of the Earth. (The white dwarf has 330,000 times the mass of the Earth but the same volume.) 1 cubic inch of white dwarf matter would weigh about 31 tons (1 cc would weigh nearly 2 tonnes).

Page 51
Workout

The Sun travels nearly 190,000 light-years during one journey around the center of the galaxy. It has made only about 22 journeys since it was born about 5 billion years ago.

Index

Numbers in italics refer to illustrations.